LENNOX Behold the Cartoons of Dracula

Sceptic Tank Press

Copyright © November 1997 Words and Cartoons Sean Lennon

Sceptic Tank Press

Designed by Sean Lennon
Published by Sceptic Tank Press
Printed by EPrint

ISBN 0-9518484-1-0

All trade enquiries to: Sceptic Tank Press
20 Alden Drive, Sutton,
Dublin 13
Telephone (01) 8323315

Other titles by Sean Lennon
Works and Quirks of the Cultured Irish
Hits and Myths: A rapid Music History from Carolan to U2

Dedicated to

CORMAC   AISLING

Contents

Introduction

1. **CINERACULA:** International Screen Star of the Undead

2. **AN ALPHABAT** More Bat-words than you have ever known

3. **HOW GRAND WAS MY GUIGNOL?** A (very) short life of Bram Stoker

4. **DRACUPUNCTURE:** The Biter gets Bitten

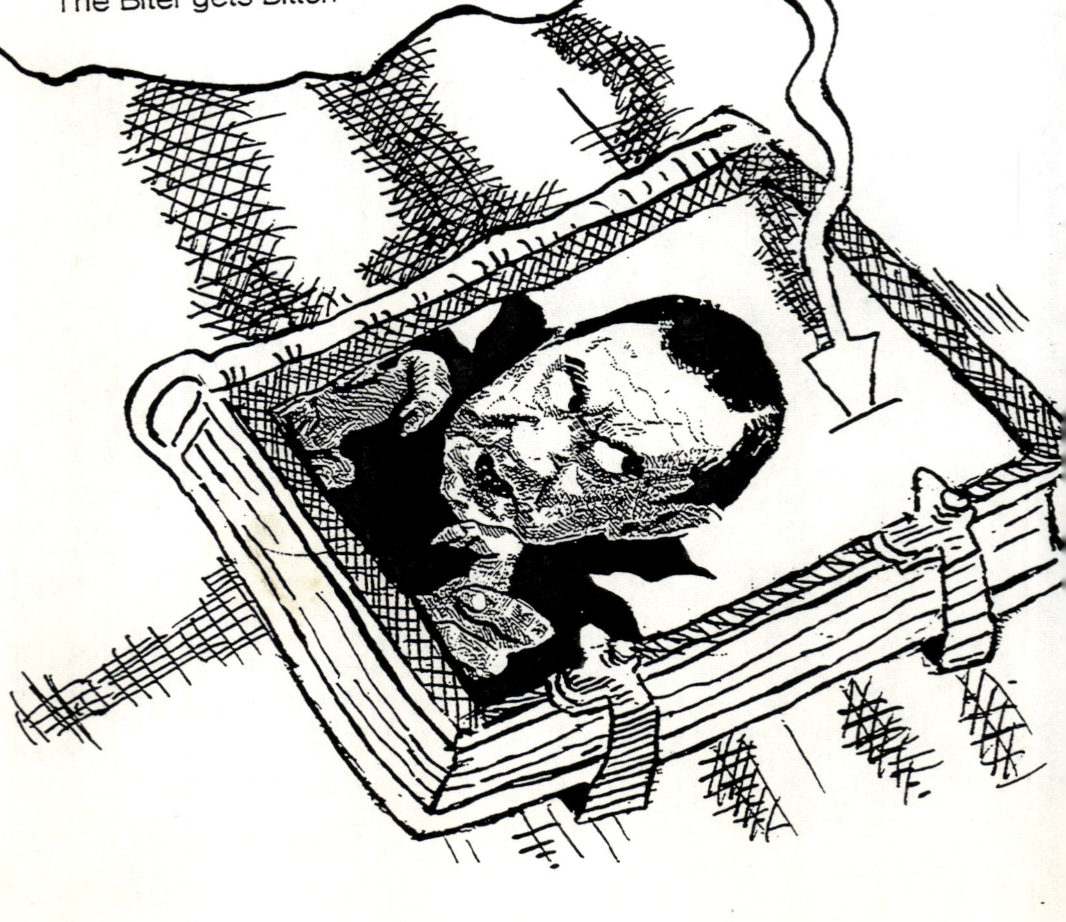

Introduction

As someone with an occupation a scant second's walk away from 15 Marino Crescent in Dublin, where Bram Stoker was born and grew up, I am regularly reminded of *Dracula's* majestic stature in the Gothic genre.

Although he was not the originator of the vampire myth in literature [a late 18th century transition from folklore to fiction saw the emergence of *The Vampyre* by John Polidori in 1819, then came James Rymer's lurid *Varney the Vampyre*, to be followed in 1872 by the great le Fanu's *Carmilla*] Bram Stoker has, for the best part of a century, been its most prominent proponent.

Dracula has never gone out of print, yet Stoker's name is comparatively unknown, never celebrated. However, with Francis Ford Coppola's cinematic rendering of the novel; the various summer schools, incorporating a Gothic collection provided by Dublin Public Libraries and assembled at Marino Library by this writer; plus the monumental biographical cartoon rehabilitation you are about to enjoy, the silence, at least for the time being, has been broken.

Perhaps now this masterpiece and Gothic mandala, which exerts an irresistible influence on film and fiction, can be seen as such, rather than the literary equivalent of a headless horseman [the missing head, of course, being the stolen property of Mr Stoker].

The inner continuum of Stoker's creation is that *Dracula* gives expression to the fears and impulses of the unconscious mind. As a cartoonist, I sometimes think the best cartoons are produced similarly, courtesy of a commerce between the conscious and the unconscious mind. The following, then, is a genuine celebration, albeit a satirical one, of Mr Stoker's achievement, conceived perhaps in the same spirit as that embodied by Ireland's greatest cult-creator.

BEHOLD THE AUTHOR-CARTOONIST OF 'BEHOLD THE CARTOONS OF DRACULA'

I. CINERACULA

F.W. MURNAU

TOD BROWNING

F.W. MURNAU'S **NOSFERATU** (1922) WITH MAX SCHRECK AS GRAF ORLOK PRESENTS THE SCREEN'S FIRST VAMPIRE. UNIVERSAL'S REPLY IS DIRECTED IN 1930 BY TOD BROWNING. DESPITE BELA LUGOSI'S SUPERB CENTRE-PIECE PERFORMANCE THE FACT THAT MOST OF THE HORROR-BEARING IN THIS **DRACULA** OCCURS OFF-SCREEN IS DISAPPOINTING. **DRACULA'S DAUGHTER** (1936) INVOLVES GLORIA HOLDEN AS A CASUALTY RATHER THAN ACTUAL DEPENDANT OF THE COUNT- WHO FAILS TO MAKE AN APPEARANCE THROUGHOUT. LON CHANEY PLAYS A PORCINE PRINCE OF DARKNESS IN **SON OF DRACULA** (43). JOHN CARRADINE'S COUNT REVERTS TO CADAVEROUS TYPE IN **HOUSE OF FRANKENSTEIN** (44) AND **HOUSE OF DRACULA** (45). LUGOSI MAKES HIS SECOND, FINAL APPEARANCE AS THE COUNT IN **BUD ABBOT AND LOU COSTELLO MEET FRANKENSTEIN** (1948). FOLLOWING A TEN-YEAR SABBATICAL AWAY FROM THE PURVIEW OF HOLLYWOOD, DRACULA RISES AGAIN FOR HAMMER FILMS **HORROR OF DRACULA** (58). DIRECTED BY TERENCE FISHER (1904-80) CHRISTOPHER LEE'S COUNT PORTRAYS A NEW SENSUALITY. EMBARKING ON 'A LONG AND PROFITABLE CAREER OF CHARNELRY' **HAMMER** ESCHEW THE GERMANIC EXPRESSIONISM OF BROWNING'S **DRACULA** AS THE SEQUELS FOLLOW IN RAPID SUCCESSION, INCLUDING THE STODGY **TASTE THE BLOOD OF DRACULA** (70); THE SUPERFICIAL **SCARS OF DRACULA** (70);

the immoderate LUST FOR A VAMPIRE (71); AND THE UNDERSTATED 'THE COUNT IS BACK WITH AN EYE FOR LONDON'S HOT PANTS' DRACULA AD 1972. HAMMER'S DEMISE IN THE SEVENTIES SIGNALS ANOTHER SABBATICAL FOR THE COUNT WHO NEVERTHELESS CONTRIVES TO KEEP HIS REPUTATION OVERGROUND WITH: AN AMERICAN TV FILM STARRING JACK PALANCE (73); ANDY WARHOL'S DRACULA (73); THE BBC'S MINI-SERIES COUNT DRACULA (74). IN THAT SAME YEAR WALTER HERZOG PAYS HIS

KLAUS KINSKI

TRIBUTE TO F.W. MURNAU IN NOSFERATU, PHANTOM DER NACHT (NOSFERATU THE VAMPYRE) WITH KLAUS KINSKI AS THE DEMONIC COUNT ORLOK. 1979 ALSO SEES A RETURN TO DRACULA BY UNIVERSAL, FRANK LANGELLA AND LAURENCE OLIVIER GIVE MEMORABLE PERFORMANCES AS THE COUNT AND VAN HELSING RESPECTIVELY. LOVE AT FIRST BITE (79) IS THE FIRST SUCCESSFUL GENRE SPOOF. EQUALLY, BUT UNINTENTIONALLY, FUNNY ADAPTATIONS INCLUDE ZOLTAN - HOUND OF DRACULA 'DRACULA'S DOG' IN AMERICA (77); BILLY THE KID MEETS DRACULA (65); THE PERCEPTIVELY SELF-CRITICAL DRACULA SUCKS (79); AND VAMPIRE DRACULA COMES TO KOBE: EVIL MAKES WOMEN BEAUTIFUL (79) WHICH CONTINUES THE GREAT CLASSIC TRADITION OF 1968'S BALEFUL DRACULA MEETS THE OUTER SPACE CHICKS. AND FINALLY THERE IS BRAM STOKER'S DRACULA (92) DIRECTED BY FRANCIS FORD COPPOLA, ONE OF THE GREAT AMERICAN WRITER DIRECTORS. IT ESTABLISHES BRAM STOKER'S CREATION AS RESPECTABLE CINEMATIC ART, AND REMAINS UNSURPASSED TODAY AS THE MAJOR FILM VERSION OF THE VAMPIRE LEGEND.

THE FIANNA FAIL ACTIVISM OF DRACULA

ORLOK'S MOUTH OR THE MACDONALDISATION OF DRACULA

"NECKst..."

THE BRIDE OF DRACULA

THE SISTER OF THE BRIDE OF DRACULA

THE THIRST OF DRACULA

ACTOR BERNARD JUKES, WHO PLAYED RENFIELD MORE THAN 4,000 TIMES, IN CHARACTER

ACTOR BERNARD JUKES OUT OF CHARACTER

THE LAST PINT OF DRACULA

THE PINT-DRINKIN' GOD-FEARIN' WAYS OF DRACULA

THE HAND OF DRACULA

THE TOPSY-TURVY WORLD OF DRACULA

2. AN ALPHABAT

From Bat Man to Male Bat, more Bat words than you have ever known.

Bataclava n.

Batbencher n.
a relatively unimportant politician

Bathander sl.
bribe

Bathful adj.
shy, modest

Batilica n.
A large Place of Worship

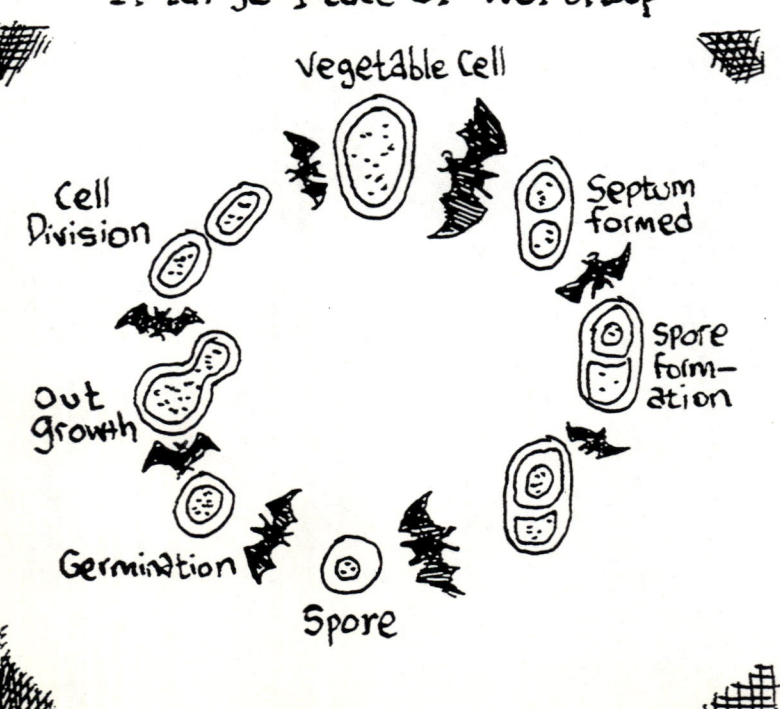

Batterium n.
pl. Batteria

Bat chain puller song-title
composed by Capt. Beefheart (above)

Bat in The USSR song-title

Bat Jokes n.
In Bat taste usually

Bat Man's Mobile n.
Car fit for a Caped Crusader

Bat Masterson sl.
Some Class of a Cowbat [Amer.]

KeBat n.
Arabian Delicacy

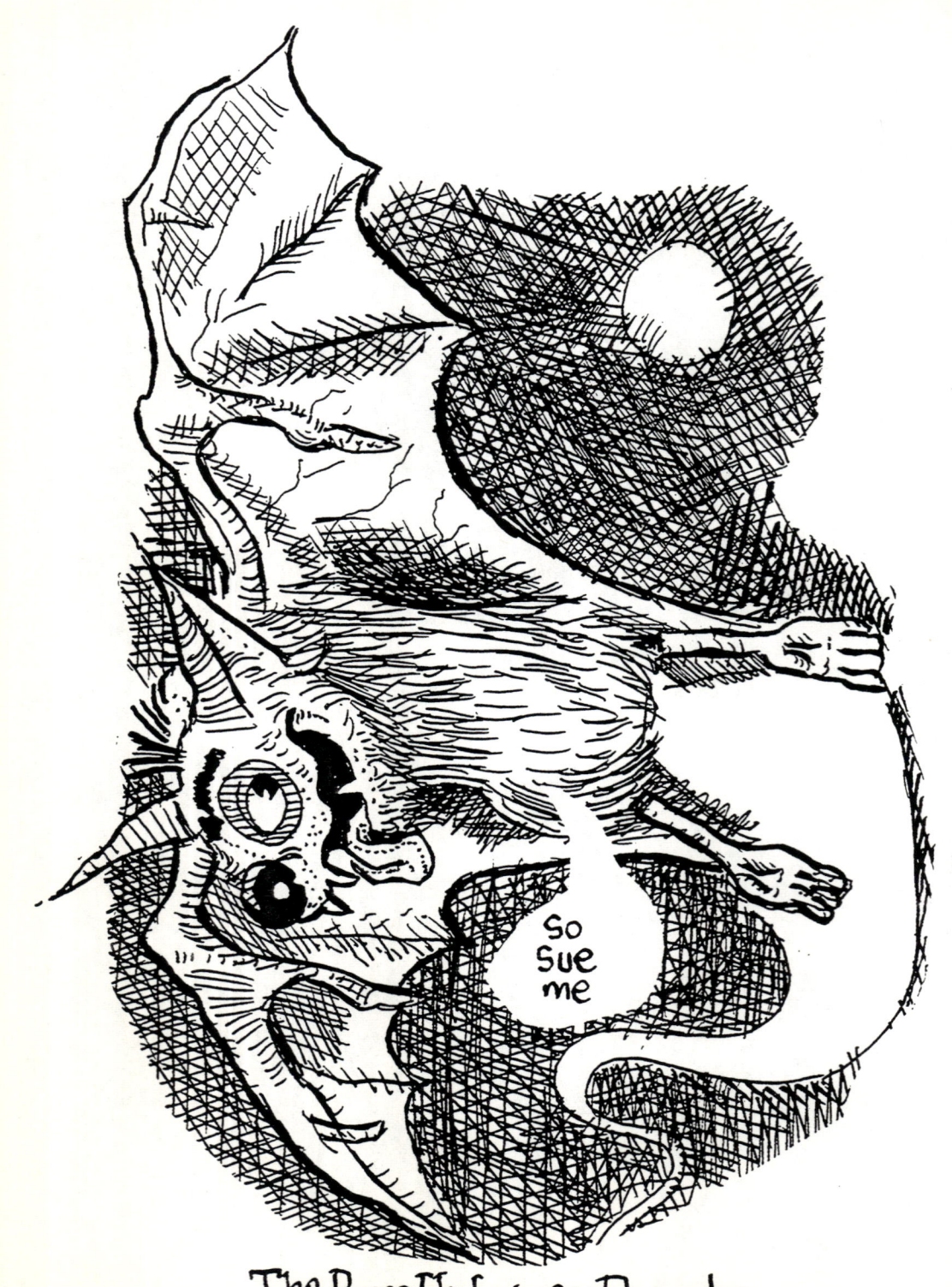

The Poor Unfortunate Batard n.
One whose father didn't quite marry his mother

BRAM STOKER IS BORN ON THE NIGHT OF 8 NOVEMBER 1847 AT 15 MARINO CRESCENT, IN THAT SEETHING HIVE OF IN- ACTIVITY WHICH IS VICTORIAN DUBLIN

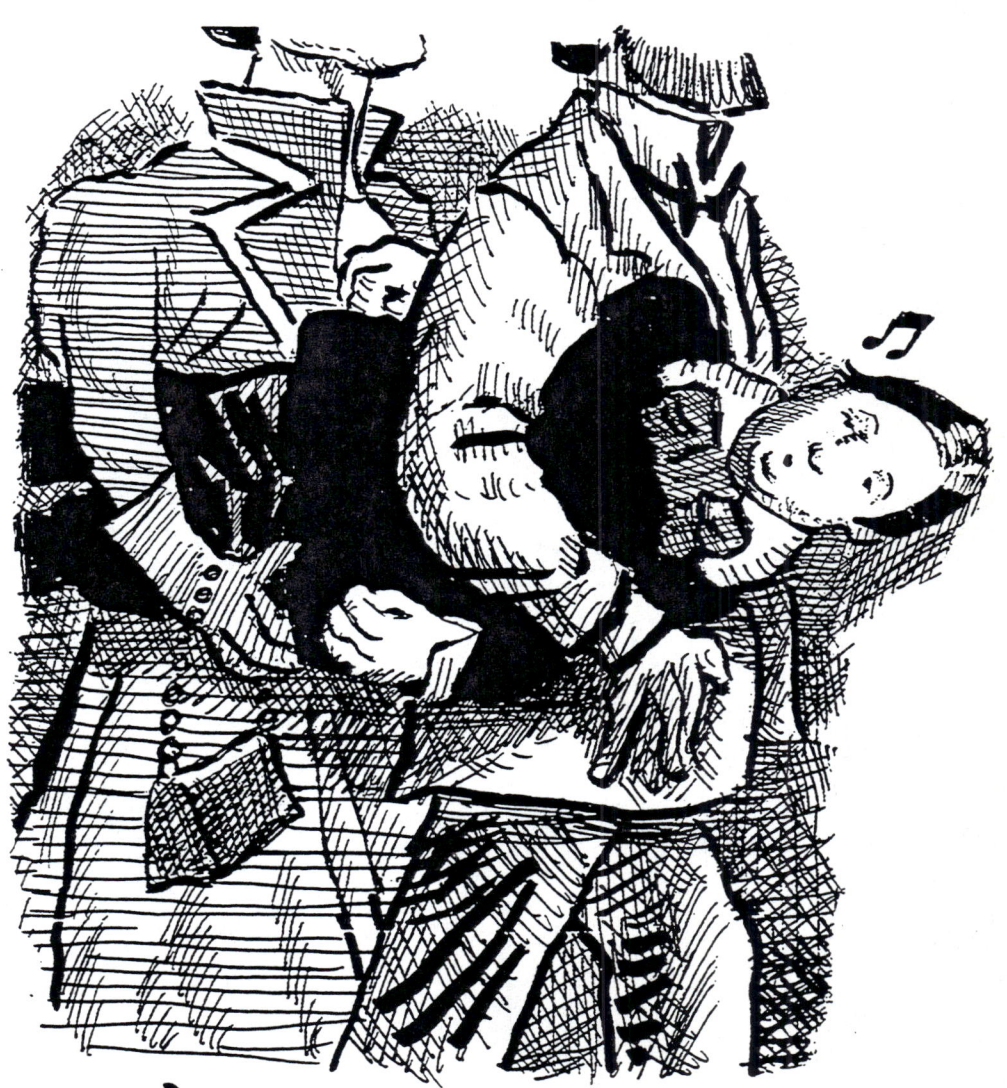

PRIOR TO ITS SPONTANEOUS REMISSION BRAM'S CHILDHOOD **MALADY** REQUIRES THAT HE BE CARRIED, FOR ROUGHLY 84 MONTHS, IN HIS PARENTS ARMS. IF BIZZARE VAPOURS, WEAKNESSES AND LIGHTNESSES IN THE HEAD (AND **LEGS**?) COME WITH THE ACQUIRED SOCIAL GRACES OF THE TIME, YOUNG STOKER IS WELL IN FASHION.

A FULLY RECOVERED BRAM ENTERS TRINITY COLLEGE IN 1863 WHERE HE ACHIEVES SIMULTANEOUS FIRSTS IN ATHLETICS AND DEBATE

BRAM FOLLOWS HIS FATHER INTO THE CIVIL SERVICE AT DUBLIN CASTLE

HE VOLUNTEERS TO WORK UNPAID AS A THEATRE CRITIC FOR THE DUBLIN EVENING MAIL, 1871.

BRAM FIRST SEES HENRY IRVING WHEN HE PLAYS CAPTAIN ABSOLUTE IN 'THE RIVALS' ON THE ROYAL STAGE, 1867

TEN YEARS LATER STOKER SEES IRVING'S HELMET WHICH CLEARLY ISN'T A PATCH ON HIS 'HAMLET' OF THE SAME TIME.

NONETHELESS, IT IS HAMLET WHICH LEAVES STOKER IN A STATE OF RAPTURE, AS HE GLOWINGLY REPORTS IN HIS THEATRE COLUMN. 'MESMERISING' PERSONAL AUDIENCES WITH THE GREAT THESPIAN FOLLOW...

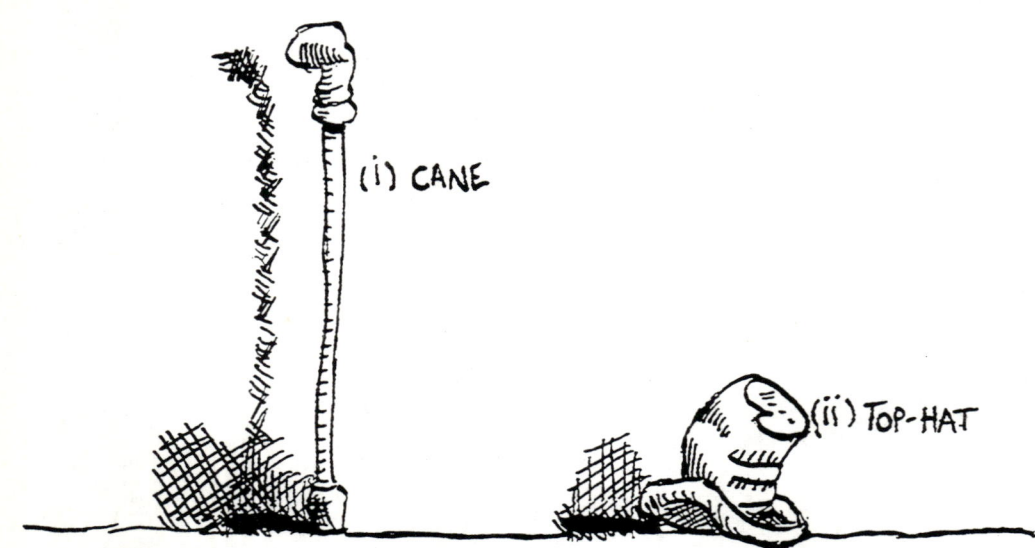

(i) CANE

(ii) TOP-HAT

BRAM ESPECIALLY ENJOYS "THE EXAGGERATED REALISM" OF DEBATE, AND PURSUES THE COMPANY OF WELL-KNOWN FASHIONABLY ATTIRED INDIVIDUALS...

(iii) MATCHING WAISTCOAT AND TAILS

(iv) FLARES

... WITH DRAMATIC. EXAGGERATED FLAIRS (SEE ABOVE) FOR THE

'A MAN'S MAN', AT 24 BRAM TAKES PAINS TO SUPPORT HIS CONTROVERSIALLY EMBROILED HERO, WALT WHITMAN

DROP-DEAD NORTHSIDE KNOCK-OUT FLORENCE BALCOMBE JILTS OSCAR WILDE AND, ON DECEMBER 4, 1878, WEDS BRAM STOKER...

SO MUCH IN LOVE. WHAT, OR WHO, COULD EVER COME BETWEEN THEM? HENRY IRVING INVITES STOKER TO MANAGE THE BUSINESS AFFAIRS OF IRVING'S OWN THEATRE, THE LONDON LYCEUM.

THE PRINCIPAL COMMENTATORS AGREE TO DIFFER BUT STOKER PROBABLY DRAWS INSPIRATION FOR THE DRACULA PERSONA FROM TWO SOURCES. THE MOST SIGNIFICANT OF THE TWO PERHAPS IS HENRY IRVING, THE 19TH CENTURY LAURENCE OLIVIER.

STOKER ALSO BECOMES FRIENDS WITH MARK TWAIN. THE HEAVY-GOING IRISHMAN IN BLACK PLAYS MR GLOOMY TO THE AMERICAN MR WHIPPY WITH THE WHITE SUIT IDÉE FIXE

COMFORTABLE WITH THE PRESSURES OF THEATRELAND HE PRODUCES A STEADY LITERARY OUTPUT, EVENTUALLY ARRIVING AT THE ONE ABOUT A CERTAIN ARISTOCRATIC TRANSYLVANIAN BLOOD-SUCKIN' ZOMBIE...

4. DRACUPUNCTURE

THE BIG MOUTH OF DRACULA

THE BOREDOM OF DRACULA/NIGHT OF THE BRAINDEAD

THE HARD LINE OF DRACULA

THE GAEILGEOIRÍ OF DRACULA

THE 1500 METRES OF DRACULA